MY 18 MONTHS OF HELL

ONE ADDICT'S HARROWING JOURNEY
INTO COCAINE ...
... AND OUT AGAIN

By
Margialee Schlachter

Copyright©2016
Margialee Schlachter

All rights reserved. No part of this book may be reproduced in any form without express written consent from the author. However, the author would be delighted to give permission for educational and rehabilitation purposes.

Although this book draws inspiration from actual events and people, the reader is reminded that this is a work of fiction, and none of the characters are intended to represent any persons living or dead.

ISBN 10: 1534837604

ISBN 13: 9781534837607

Printed in the United States of America
By

G

G J Publishing
515 Cimarron Circle, Suite 323
Loudon TN 37774
865-567-5394
www.neilans.com

Chapter 1

Speeding along on the hilly country road, I was thinking to myself, "Brady LaLone, you can lose that police car that's been chasing you through two counties for over two hours." But then up ahead I saw lights from another patrol car, and it was crossways in the road.

"Ah damn, they got me!" I pulled to a stop, put the car in park and turned off the key. I put my hands in the air and waited. I realized the jig was up.

An officer hurried to my door and ordered me out of the car. When I complied he said, "Put your hands behind your back," and proceeded to cuff me. That done he pushed me from behind and I went down, sprawling in the gravel at the side of the road. He ordered me to lie still and not move. He then began searching the car.

I wasn't too worried as I had ditched the cocaine along the way. I figured the most he could get me for would be failure to stop. My dealer had always told us to lose the drugs if we were under surveillance. I'd done just that so didn't think I was in serious trouble.

When the officer did not find any illegal substances in the car, he came up behind me and gave me a swift stomp to the head with his police issued boot, as I lay defenseless on the ground. I could tell he was a rookie cop, and he was about to teach me a lesson. My face slid along in the gravel as he kicked me a second and third time. Now I realized I was in *serious* trouble, because he wasn't going to stop! Several more stomps and I knew I'd be unconscious.

The siren from the police car in front of us came on for a second and then went off. I heard a woman officer say, "That's enough! Any more and you will be taking him back to the station in a body bag!"

By now I was bleeding from my face, nose and ears. My head was swelling and my brain felt like it had been used for a soccer ball.

The female officer shined a light on me and I heard her say, "For god's sake Shultz, you really got carried away this time. I know you found no drugs and I have to tell you the owner of this car isn't this kid, you got the wrong man! How do you plan to explain this to Lieutenant Williams on the desk tonight? When you arrive at the station, you'd better get this guy downstairs to the men's washroom and get him cleaned up fast."

The officer who had kicked me said, "Get up and get in the back seat, Mr. Smart Guy!"

I struggled to stand, let alone walk, but did manage to do as I was told on my own. The police station was about ten miles away but it seemed even farther because my body ached all over from the beating he'd inflicted on me. When we finally arrived, Officer Schultz drove under the building into the parking garage. He stopped the car and told me to get out.

We walked toward the washroom in the back. He was behind me, which made me fearful, but once we got inside, he took the handcuffs off and ordered me to clean myself up.

I stepped to the sink while he walked over to the paper towel dispensary. When he saw it was empty he proceeded to slam it with his fist. He said to me, "Start cleaning up, I'll be right back!"

I looked at myself in the mirror and barely recognized my face. Swollen and bloodied ... I was a mess. As I bent down in front of the sink and turned on the water, I realized I still had my cell phone in my right boot. I always carried it there so as not to forget it. I reached into my boot, pulled it out, and holding it up, took a picture of my battered face. I slipped it back into my boot as I heard the officer returning from down the hall with the paper towels. I splashed my face with water and he tossed me a package of towels to dry myself off. Because I had so much blood down the front of my shirt he ordered me to turn my tee shirt inside out and to tuck my coat collar under. I did both and we headed to the admitting room upstairs on the second floor.

Standing in front of the officer on duty, Lieutenant Williams, I waited for whatever was coming next. He didn't say a word as he began to shuffle through some papers and soon passed them to me to sign. I took the pen and signed where he indicated.

The lieutenant said, "You can make one phone call, son, then you will be put in a holding cell until you are released."

I walked to the telephone on the wall and phoned Walt Young, my roommate Rick's Uncle. He was the only person I could think of who would help me. Rick had been in a scrape with the law a week earlier, and he had called Walt to come to his rescue. Walt was well familiar with the police and he was street smart about the law. I told him where I was and that I needed him to come and get me released from jail.

I sat in the cell for about an hour. I could barely keep from upchucking because of the horrible smell. The entire space reeked of booze, body odor and puke from previous inmates. I had never felt that much pain in all my nineteen years, and the time seemed to crawl by. Finally Uncle Walt arrived and I was led back in front of Lt. Williams. He looked down at me, shuffling through the papers once again looking for a release form for me to sign. While he was doing that I showed Uncle Walt my cell phone picture. He took one look at my battered face and bloody clothes and I could see that he was madder than hell.

Walt spoke to Lt. Williams and said, "You might want to see this," and proceeded to show him the picture on my cell phone."

Lt. Williams looked disgusted and was trying to find his voice and what to say. Uncle Walt said simply, "You might want to lose those papers!"

It didn't take the Lieutenant long to respond, "You're free to go son." He handed me the keys to the vehicle we'd left along the side of the road.

There had been no mention of bond money, just as Uncle Walt expected. This wasn't his first rodeo!

When we got outside Uncle Walt said, "You did the right thing taking that photo. I don't think we'll hear any more about this incident. We'll stop by the house so you can get to bed, son, I'm sure you are feeling a lot of pain. But, I'd like to know, what were you doing driving Rick's car tonight?

I answered, "I saw that mine had a flat tire just as I was about to make a delivery, and Rick told me to take his; he said I could change my tire when I got back."

Walt nodded. "Rick can go with me to pick up his car. You took the whipping that he would have gotten had they caught him. He said the cops've been watching him come and go. and tonight was bound to happen."

•••••••

In the weeks following that night I began to have seizures. They were happening often and lasting longer each time. But was I smart enough to quit taking cocaine? NO!

Chapter 2

This might not be worth a darn to read but I need to get it off my chest. When my life started as the youngest of five children, my family loved me, Brady La Lone, from the day I was born. I had absolutely no reason to become a druggie. Good parents and four older siblings to guide me through life.

And yet, it happened.

You get the picture by now, the LaLone Family. A middle class life with a loving mother Carol and a hard working father Sam, who supported us by working long hours and was absent from home a lot because of it. Not so bad a life really. Mother didn't work outside the home but she had plenty to do raising five kids. We weren't the Brady bunch but close to it. I never doubted the love we all shared in our home. Mom supported and encouraged us in our school activities and was always willing to drive us to them and come pick us up afterwards. I had two older brothers, Gary and Zack and two older sisters, Sandy and Katie. They did a good job of keeping me in line and out of trouble, most of the time.

By the time I came along my folks were making a good living raising the family so one more child wasn't that big a deal. It hadn't always been like that, as my folks were young and had started out with nothing. My dad worked hard to build his trucking business, and had a lot of ups and downs in the early years. He also was a mechanic so worked long hours to keep his equipment in good working order.

Because Dad was away from home a lot, our family had more meals without him than with him. Mom didn't like it but learned to expect to feed us and put his meal in the microwave for later.

My first five years were memorable because of all the attention I received from Mom and my older siblings. My brothers and sisters were all in school so I had Mother's full attention. She and I spent a lot of time at the grade school because she volunteered there several days a week. By the time I started school I knew some of the teachers and the principal by name and they knew me. I liked school and usually looked forward to it.

Like I said earlier I learned to behave in the presence of older grownups, so I rarely got punished for being a brat. I don't remember ever being spanked. My folks weren't into physical punishment; if any of their children needed to be reminded of poor behavior, they usually withheld something we were looking forward to and thus we were excluded from that event or privilege. By having the older kids to clue me in I avoided a lot of situations that could have been tough on me.

We had the usual family reunions and picnics and short vacations in the summertime when school was out. My sisters were into cheerleading and my brothers were into sports - all the normal things for the kids in our neighborhood.

Chapter 3

When I was ten years old I got a dirt bike. I loved that bike. My brother Zack was sixteen and had his driver's license. His best friend Mike also had a bike and they would load up the three bikes on a trailer and off we would go to ride the trails about fifteen miles from our home. Such fun we had on many an afternoon that lasted into the night. When darkness arrived that meant we were to end our riding, load up the bikes, and return home. I always felt a part of the pack because my brother treated me like one of the gang. He never made fun of me or put me down. In my mind I was sixteen too and tried to act like a teenager.

I got interested in baseball at the age of twelve. I tried out for catcher and got picked by the coach to play that position. I was so excited and from then on that's all I did ... talk and play baseball. My sister Katie would throw for me so I could improve my technique. We spent a lot of time out in the driveway. Every game we played some one from my family would be in the stands encouraging our home team to a victory.

I played for two years and started the third thinking I'd play until I graduated; but my interest in the sport came to a sudden halt when one night after the game a new pitcher,

Chad, asked me to stay so he could practice his curve ball. I loved helping anyone that loved the sport like I did, so after the field cleared and the other players were in the locker room, Chad and I practiced for almost an hour. When we finally called it a night, I headed for home on my bike and Chad went to the locker room to shower.

Chad called me later that night and shared with me some shocking and nearly unbelievable news regarding what he'd witnessed when he had walked into the locker room a few hours earlier. He had not been expected, that's for sure ... when he entered the locker room, he found one of the players performing a sex act on Coach Hayes! Chad backed out of the room quietly undetected and hurried home in disbelief. He had held Coach Hayes in high regard as his mentor and as a good moral person. We both did. I couldn't get to sleep that night. I tossed and turned just trying to wrap my mind around this devastating news.

Coach Hayes had been at our school coaching and teaching for over ten years. He had been a trophy winner in his college years and well thought of for his contributions to our school. He had kids of his own who were in college.

I was disappointed in the coach and decided that I'd never be put in that situation or be witness to such an act. I told the assistant coach I was quitting the game the next day. He questioned me for an explanation and I found it hard to explain my reasons. I finally just said that I was tired of the game. Chad found me later after school was out and said that he too had quit the team. Looking back now I realize we were at an age that found it unimaginable to get past that kind of behavior on the part of the coach we'd looked up to and admired. I couldn't talk about what had happened with my brothers because they had graduated and were out of the house. My youngest sister Katie was a senior about to graduate high school and I was sure she'd think I was over reacting to quit the team, so I kept it inside and shared my emotions with no one.

Several weeks later Chad joined the track team and moved on in sports, following track as his two older brothers had done in previous years. He excelled like the talented champions in his family. We never discussed the incident again but, for me, I could never forget or forgive the coach.

Chapter 4

By the time I was in my junior year at high school, my oldest brother Gary had begun driving a truck for Dad and had his own apartment with his girl friend Polly. My oldest sister Sandy was attending her last year in college, completing a BA degree. Her last two years we hardly saw her as she lived and worked on campus fifty miles from home. My brother Zack was a senior and planning to graduate that June and to attend a trade school in the fall. That left my sister Katie and me as the only two kids still in school and living at home.

I began to notice girls from afar. I didn't approach them because I was so shy, but I did discover a new girl in class that year. Sally Click had transferred to my school from a small town in Idaho. Her father's job had moved him and his family to our town. Now that I was no longer interested in baseball and had given up my dirt bike riding, I spent my free time checking out Sally. She had long black hair and was a really attractive girl. I finally got up the courage to introduce myself, and followed her between classes to her locker. I asked her how she liked our town and she said, "I've only been here two weeks and haven't had a chance to look around. I hurry home from school to look after my eight year old brother Lance. Both my parents work till five p.m."

I asked her if she'd like to go to a movie on a Saturday or Sunday and to my surprise she said, "That would be great." Since I wasn't old enough to drive a car, we walked to the theater on our first date. I met Sally's folks Hal and Anita when I picked her up and they were a very friendly couple. We chatted about her having had to leave all her friends behind. I told her that I'd introduce her around to my friends and she'd fit right in at our school in no time.

Sally's mom asked me what I did in my free time away from school and I told her that on weekends I usually went down to the truck yard and helped my Dad wash and grease trucks and to listen to the drivers talk about some of their experiences driving in the city traffic. I explained to her what a tough dangerous job it was if you weren't properly trained for it. I couldn't think of anything else I wanted to do but drive truck someday in my future.

Sally and I found it easy to talk about our lives and she became my first girlfriend. My Mom liked her and she was at our house a lot over the next year. We dated all through our senior year but drifted apart when she left for college that fall. Her folks had been planning for Sally to continue her education after high school and she had applied to several colleges. We weren't serious in our relationship but I'd hoped we could continue to be in touch while she was away at school. It didn't happen that way; she met a fellow, Stephen Rhodes, the first week she arrived and that was the end of us. I think that happens to a lot of people when they separate and one goes off to a university and one stays behind.

Chapter 5

In my senior year I found a wonderful teacher, Bill Wynn, who taught welding in shop class. He really made the class seem interesting. I wanted to learn all that I could about that trade so I could help my Dad someday in his trucking business.

I graduated High School in June and would turn nineteen that fall. My school counselor helped me decide what I wanted to do after graduation. I didn't want to go on to college. A trade school seemed more sensible to me. Welding was my choice and I could get a certificate in nine months and be out earning my own money. That was my goal ... to be self supporting and making my own living.

I still thought about truck driving, hauling steel for my Dad, but that would be down the road when I was older. In the meanwhile, I'd get this experience of welding until that day arrived.

I enrolled at NU in Nashville, Tennessee. I scanned the newspaper for a furnished room to rent, looking for a location close to the university campus. I soon found a room available within two miles. I met one of the sweetest little ole ladies, Maggie Barnett, and moved into her home. The evening meal was included in my weekly rent ... what a deal!

I started my search for a part time job the first day as soon as I unpacked. Albertson's grocery store had an ad in the paper for night clerks to stock shelves. I applied and got hired to start immediately that evening. My classes were five days a week from ten o'clock to three thirty so I had an hour before clocking in at Albertson's. Mrs. Barnett would put my evening meal into the microwave and I would eat it after getting home from my job at the grocery store. My work schedule was for five nights a week, giving me weekends off to study or relax.

When I'd only been in class for a week I realized welding wasn't for me. I just couldn't see myself welding day after day for the rest of my life. However, I'd paid a chunk of money up front for the course so felt I had to see it through to the end. Nine months would pass by quickly, I thought, and I would always be able to use the knowledge someday.

I liked the instructor, Mr. Powell. He was a very patient man with all the students. He told us right from day one that if we didn't understand to ask questions because that's how we would learn. I took notes and really tried to learn as much as possible.

We learned that metals are all different, so we would have to vary the thickness of each weld and select the correct tools every time. It was all new to most of the class but I'd helped my dad weld on his trailers, so some of it came easily to me. Mr. Powell said, "I can see you've been exposed to some of this son, and the rest will come in time; be patient."

Chapter 6

My time on the weekends was my own to sleep in, relax, and to call home. I missed my family but it was time to leave the nest and to be on my own.

My two roommates, Lance Story and Nick Adams, were new in town like I was and we started checking out Nashville. None of us were old enough to drink and hang out in the bars, so we would go fishing together or watch sports on TV. We became good friends right away. None of us had a lot of money so our evenings were spent sitting around the dining room table playing poker or board games.

Our landlady Mrs. Barnett was so good to us, we became like family. The weeks rolled by and the holidays arrived. I went home to spend a few days with my folks and my sister Katie. She was going to college but still living at home. My older brothers, Gary and Zack and other sister, Sandy, came for Christmas. It was so good to be with my whole family. I had missed them while I was away at school. They had all moved on in their lives. Happy faces and healthy family were gathered at home and my Mom couldn't have been happier or prouder of her kids.

I returned to school and work after the holidays with a new attitude. I was determined to see this through and grow up a little ... I hoped. June and graduation wouldn't be far away. Time passed by and I did enjoy my stay in Nashville. Lance changed jobs several times while living at the rooming house but I know he liked the friendships he'd formed with Nick and me. The three of us still hung around together on the weekends. I keep in touch with both of them to this day.

Graduation Day was approaching and I was planning to head back home. I wanted my independence to continue but wasn't sure just how I could afford living on my own. I'd gotten lucky living in the rooming house with my friends but wasn't sure what it would be like back home. Maggie Barnett had been like a grandmother to Lance, Nick and me, and I had a hard time saying goodbye to her. I promised to write.

I left that day feeling good about the friends I'd made and how special they were to me.

Chapter 7

So much can change at the age of nineteen. Being away from home had been hard on me but it also helped me grow up and figure out things for myself about life and how to survive.

I arrived back to my Mother's waiting arms and quickly unpacked the bags with all my stuff. After resting up for a couple days I ventured out to see if I could find any old classmates or neighborhood chums. I started looking at the local gym. There I ran into Rick Wagner from High School. He wasn't a close friend but we had been in some classes together. Rick had been a quiet kid in high school. Not active in sports or school activities, he was a loner, an only child, raised by a single mother who owned her own business. His Mother, Anita Wagner, worked long hours and he was very much on his own after school and on weekends. He would sometimes help out in her restaurant when Anita needed extra help with deliveries or if a worker didn't show up for work.

Anita would always say, "Rick needs to be a kid for as long as he can be. He'll have time to work after he graduates from school." Well, that happened and the week after all the parties and celebrating, he found a small house he could afford and moved into it.

He asked me what I'd been up to after graduation. We started talking and he told me about the house he was renting. He occupied one upstairs bedroom, and had rented the second one to his chum Omar. I didn't know Omar. Rick had met him after school and they had become friends.

He went on to say that if I needed a place to live, he had a third room available. I said yes, I'd take it, and soon I moved my stuff into the basement bedroom at Rick's place on Grover Street.

Unknown to me, Rick was now involved in the drug world, and Omar was his link; soon enough he would be my link as well.

The trouble that followed was my own fault for making such a hasty decision to take Rick up on his offer of renting a room in his house.

Chapter 8

I found a job at a service garage the first week; just something to pay my bills and the rent.

I was not prepared for the next chapter in my life at Rick's. I found out he was dealing drugs for his living. This was not on my radar! Never in my wildest imagination did I think he'd be involved in the drug world. I was such a greenie. Now I needed to figure out a way to get out of this living situation I had so hastily gotten myself into.

Rick and Omar were cutting cocaine on the kitchen table several nights a week. When I'd get off work, that's what I would walk in on. I started looking for another place to live. I didn't want the cops to raid the house and cart me off to jail just for my association with them.

I struggled to get myself out of there, but working my day job didn't leave me much time to look for another place.

My two housemates were not using the cocaine but had quite a large clientele, judging by all the dope I saw being divided there in the kitchen, night after night. At least they didn't have people coming to the house. Rick delivered the drugs so there'd be less chance of anybody knowing the location of their operation.

Week after week went by as I tried not to let on how helpless I was feeling. I thought about going back home but Mom was now working as a secretary at the grade school. With all the kids grown and out of the house she needed to be busy and get on with enjoying her life. She felt needed at her job. She wouldn't have said no to my moving back home, but I wanted my independence. All my siblings were getting on with their lives and I wanted that for me too, but just how to achieve it was beyond my grasp. I needed help but didn't know which way to turn to get it.

Not happy about my job or living in a drug house, I really was depressed. One night Omar and Rick, along with a couple of their friends, offered me a free sample. I joined them in trying a line of coke. After all, it was free and it would just be the one time. At least that is what I thought.

Why I lowered myself to do that, I'll never know. I have no excuses for my actions. Getting high did lift my spirits, so for a while the world didn't seem so bad. But before long I was hooked on the damn stuff! I began looking forward to it and soon stopped thinking about moving out.

I'd go to work every day but then hurry home to get high. Soon I learned that the *samples* were no longer *free*. Having a drug habit now meant *"Paying to play."* My service job wasn't paying enough money to support my expenses of rent, food, gas, insurance and now the drugs I was hooked on. What a sucker I'd become to get myself into this situation.

Chapter 9

Now I couldn't go home to Mom and Dad's very often as I was always either high or needing to get high. They could tell I had changed when they saw how jittery I'd become, with a "Gotta go" attitude whenever I was around them. I was no longer the happy go lucky kid they'd known and raised. Even when around my siblings, I was now always in a hurry, afraid they'd give me the heat on my lifestyle, and I couldn't explain it to myself let alone try to talk about it to others.

Unhappy but hooked and caught up in a world of hurt, not knowing what to do or which way to turn, I struggled with the way of life I had gotten myself into.

Rick knew how to manipulate suckers like me into doing his drug deliveries. I became one of his "Drug Runners" over the next year and a half. I had several close calls with the police. They were watching the house and with us always making deliveries after dark it was only a matter of time until one of us got busted with some kind of substance on us.

I got fired from my job at Wally's service garage. I couldn't be up all hours of the night and still show up for work on time come morning. Wally couldn't depend on me so had to let me go. That was one of my lowest days when I got fired in front of the crew at work. I left and went home to get high on cocaine.

I went on a real bender and it brought on my first seizure.

Chapter 10

This brings us back to the opening chapter in my story and my trying to outrun the rookie cop. I had been planning to make a delivery that night but I had to ditch the dope.

With no job, I had to deliver drugs to support my habit. Sleep all day then prowl and deliver the drugs at night - that was my mode of operation. I continued on this path of destruction for twelve months.

My seizures, meanwhile, were getting worse.

One night I went into a *grand mal* seizure in front of Rick and Omar. I was lying on the couch in the living room and started twitching and frothing at the mouth. They had no idea of what to do for me so they did nothing but stand there in shock and watch me. They told me later that I had turned gray and my eyes had rolled back in my head, and it had scared them out of their wits.

After some time I came out of the seizure, drained and exhausted. I opened my eyes and saw them staring at me. They finally decided to take me to the hospital. I managed to get myself into the car and Omar drove straight to the emergency room at midnight. The intern on duty asked me what I had taken and before I even answered, he said, "Don't try to lie to me, I've seen it all."

I told him it was cocaine. He said, "That drug is causing your seizures."

I told him that I'd recently been kicked in the head and asked, "Could that be causing it?"

He said, "No, we see this happening a lot in here in people who are taking cocaine and heroin. The *grand mal* is the worst. One day, you could die from it. This is serious, son, and you need to know the facts." He paused to let that sink in, then added, "You're not even twenty-one years old and the road you're on is a dead end. Literally."

He released me and told me to go home and get some sleep. "Think about what I've said. What you do now is up to you."

I was so drained from that ordeal, I slept for two days. But I couldn't give up the coke. It had a hold of me and I was hooked!

Chapter 11

My turning point came in spite of my delay in making the decision to help myself. One night I was helping a friend of Omar's, Sammy Goodwin, take apart his motorcycle engine. We were in his garage working until two a.m., when we finally finished and called it a night. Sammy closed and locked the garage door and I headed for my car parked in his driveway.

I started to stumble as a seizure was coming on. I went down on the cement on all fours. Sammy was in shock at what was happening to me. He had no idea how to help. Finally, remembering he had a screwdriver in his back pocket and fearing I'd swallow my tongue, he placed it between my teeth. The seizure was so violent and I bit down so hard, I knocked out a lot of my teeth. He was terrified but stayed with me through the seizure until it eased up.

Soon I was back into another one so he placed the screwdriver back in my mouth again. This time my throat took the blunt of the tool. I continued to froth and flail until the seizure finally subsided. I was weak and limp lying there on the cement. This had been the worst seizure I'd ever had. My mouth was bleeding a lot. Sammy got me up on my feet, walked me to his car, and drove straight to the emergency room at Cedars Hospital.

I was in surgery for several hours. The surgeon worked on me until seven a.m. My family hurried to the hospital after Sammy called and told them he thought I was dying.

Over the next few days I was kept sedated. My mom sat by my bed day and night crying and praying. I'd try to talk but couldn't get the words to come out. Slowly I could feel the drugs leaving my body. The soreness in my mouth began to ease up and I could speak out loud.

What a mess I'd made of myself! I felt so ashamed of what I'd become, it was hard to face my loved ones.

My dad sat with me whenever Mom took a break. My whole family was so worried about me. My sisters came and when they saw my face, both Sandy and Katie starting sobbing. I didn't look like the little brother they knew. They all loved me and were there for me when I needed their support.

My brother Zack stayed all night with me on the third day after surgery. I finally felt like talking and I knew he wouldn't judge me. I opened up and spilled my guts out to him. He sat quietly and let me talk, knowing this was what I needed; just getting it out there and moving forward away from that drug pit.

I badly wanted my life back.

He let me finish speaking, then when I wound down he said simply, "I've got a mirror here. Do you want to see what you look like?"

I took the mirror and couldn't speak. I saw one inch cuts on both corners of my mouth that the surgeon had made so he could fix the damage in my throat. My face was chalk white and when I opened my mouth wide, I could see spaces where many teeth, *seven* to be exact, were missing! Tears welled up in my eyes and I said, *"I'll never touch it again, Zack."*

He leaned over and wrapped his arms around me in a tight embrace. We both cried as I made that vow to my brother and to myself: *I was finished with drugs*!

My dad said that I could come back home when I was released from the hospital; he also emphasized that I would need to disassociate myself from all the people I'd been hanging around with who were still selling and using drugs.

I took his advice and was so thankful to have my parents' home as a safe haven for my recovery. Zack picked up my personal things and my car from Rick's place for me so I wouldn't have to see anyone from my old lifestyle.

I spent the next several months healing my mind and my body at home with my family loving me and supporting me. They wouldn't let me self-destruct in the drug world.

Oh, and I also went to a dentist for bridges to replace the teeth I had lost.

Chapter 12

When I was no longer suffering from the surgery and the drugs, I had a long talk with my dad about my future. He said, "You haven't had a seizure for a long time. Perhaps you could drive for me now, if that's what you want to do. You will have to stay off drugs and be tested for epilepsy every six months."

I gratefully accepted his terms. I turned twenty-one that fall and started working for him. I drove an eight year old red Kenworth truck, hauling coiled steel from the docks where it had been brought in by boat, and delivering it to the processing plants for making cars. It is one thing that I'm good at and I have continued doing it for the past fifteen years.

I went for the seizure testing for the first two years and I always tested clean. I have had a safe driving record with no tickets and no accidents. I also want to add that I have no criminal record. Guess they forgot to turn in the police record that night long ago when I was a punk kid trying to outrun the cops. It would have meant no truck driving for a living for me and for that, (and for Uncle Walt), I'm so truthfully thankful.

I saved my money and finally purchased my own truck, a two year old charcoal gray Peterbilt, after driving for my dad for five years. It was a big purchase for me, and a big responsibility. I now had truck payments, plus expenses for fuel, tires, insurance, and repairs. I was facing all the headaches that come with vehicle ownership.

My dad is happy to have given me my chance to prove myself and I have passed his expectations. I'll try to never let him down. With that said, my life probably wouldn't have turned out this well without the support of all who love me.

Chapter 13

I want to add this final chapter to my story as I live it today.

I met my loving wife, Robyn Ann, through friends. We were both in our early thirties and started a flirtation that developed into a strong friendship and then into a long lasting relationship. She was the girl for me and just who I needed in my life. I felt I had to share my past history on drugs with her.

When I told her about my eighteen months of Hell, she listened and decided to stick around in spite of it. I asked her to marry me and she said, *Yes*!

No long engagement for us; we began planning the wedding for Christmastime and within three months we had tied the knot with her family and mine all around us.

Robyn Ann is the most precious thing that's ever happened to me and I will cherish her until the day I'm no longer drawing a breath. She treats me like a king and I hope we can grow old together sitting out on the porch holding hands in our rocking chairs.

Author's Note

I have over the years been interested in stories about drug misuse. There are many ways both kids and adults can get caught up in drugs. Sometimes it is an inability to let go of the high caused by prescriptions written for valid injuries or illnesses. Sometimes such illnesses and injuries are faked in order to persuade a physician to write more prescriptions. Teenagers, too young to purchase alcohol, often cave in to peer pressure to get high, finding creative ways to obtain such substances without going to either a medical or back alley source – such as taking pills from a parent's pain medication stash. Adults can get creative, too, going across borders into Mexico or Canada to get drugs restricted in their own country.

Speaking from my own experience, I never thought I was the sort of person to use drugs, but I found out how addictive these substances can be. I was caught up in cocaine after just one experience with it.

I was lucky that my *grand mal* seizure was so severe. It sent me to the hospital with so much physical damage that I had to step away from my destructive lifestyle. And I was especially lucky to have the support of my loving family.

I would like to say in closing this story, that if any of you or your friends find yourselves caught up in substance abuse, be it drugs, alcohol or whatever, there is *always hope.*

In my case, I don't take the credit for getting out of it on my own. A lot of good loving people were praying and supporting me. But I'd had all that and still threw it away for cocaine.

They tell me that I have an *addictive personality*, which is why the drug got hold of me so easily. However, I had no way to know that, until I made that fateful decision to try cocaine "just one time." I have also learned that alcohol is my enemy.

I leave it all alone now, and get high just having my life back.

I want to leave you with this thought: You have a *choice* to make on how you want to live your life.

I chose to live mine *without drugs*.

I hope you will, too.

Marge Schlachter
2000 Ramar Rd.
Lot #460
Bullhead City AZ
84442

37043457R00021

Made in the USA
San Bernardino, CA
08 August 2016